SUPER SANDCASTLE

It's the Alphabet!

It's N!

Oona Gaarder-Juntti

Consulting Editor, Diane Craig, M.A./Reading Specialist

ABDO
Publishing Company

Published by ABDO Publishing Company, 8000 West 78th Street, Edina, Minnesota 55439. Copyright © 2010 by Abdo Consulting Group, Inc. International copyrights reserved in all countries. No part of this book may be reproduced in any form without written permission from the publisher. Super SandCastle™ is a trademark and logo of ABDO Publishing Company.

Printed in the United States.

♲ PRINTED ON RECYCLED PAPER

Editor: Katherine Hengel
Content Developer: Nancy Tuminelly
Cover and Interior Design and Production: Kelly Doudna, Mighty Media
Photo Credits: AbleStock, iStockphoto (Jani Bryson, Peggy De Meue), Shutterstock

Library of Congress Cataloging-in-Publication Data
Gaarder-Juntti, Oona, 1979-
  It's N! / Oona Gaarder-Juntti.
     p. cm. -- (It's the Alphabet!)
  ISBN 978-1-60453-601-0
  1. English language--Alphabet--Juvenile literature. 2. Alphabet books--Juvenile literature. I. Title.
  PE1155.G2938 2010
  421'.1--dc22
  〈E〉
                            2009021023

Super SandCastle™ books are created by a team of professional educators, reading specialists, and content developers around five essential components—phonemic awareness, phonics, vocabulary, text comprehension, and fluency—to assist young readers as they develop reading skills and strategies and increase their general knowledge. All books are written, reviewed, and leveled for guided reading, early reading intervention, and Accelerated Reader® programs for use in shared, guided, and independent reading and writing activities to support a balanced approach to literacy instruction.

About SUPER SANDCASTLE™

Bigger Books for Emerging Readers
Grades K–4

Created for library, classroom, and at-home use, Super SandCastle™ books support and engage young readers as they develop and build literacy skills and will increase their general knowledge about the world around them. Super SandCastle™ books are an extension of SandCastle™, the leading preK–3 imprint for emerging and beginning readers. Super SandCastle™ features a larger trim size for more reading fun.

Let Us Know
Super SandCastle™ would like to hear your stories about reading this book. What was your favorite page? Was there something hard that you needed help with? Share the ups and downs of learning to read. We want to hear from you! Send us an e-mail.

sandcastle@abdopublishing.com

Contact us for a complete list of SandCastle™, Super SandCastle™, and other nonfiction and fiction titles from ABDO Publishing Company.

www.abdopublishing.com • 8000 West 78th Street
Edina, MN 55439 • 800-800-1312 • 952-831-1632 fax

Aa Bb Cc Dd Ee

Ff Gg Hh Ii Jj Kk

Ll Mm Nn Oo Pp

Qq Rr Ss Tt Uu Vv

Ww Xx Yy Zz

The Letter Nn

The letter n in
American Sign Language

N and n can also look like

Nn **Nn** Nn Nn Nn Nn

4

The letter **n** is a consonant.

It is the 14th letter of the alphabet.

Some words start with **n**.

noodles

nest

nickel

Natalie

Natalie nibbles noodles next to a nest full of new nickels.

Some words have **n** in the middle.

fence   pencil

Andy   Vanessa

Andy and his friend Vanessa find many orange pencils under the fence.

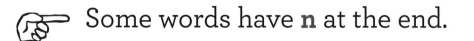 Some words have **n** at the end.

moon

lion

Kevin

Kevin can ride to the moon on a lion and then return in ten days.

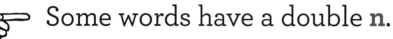 Some words have a double **n**.

inn

bunny

Jenny and her bunny buy
dinner at the inn
for a penny.

penny

12

n as in spri**ng** and dri**nk**

monkey

A k or g after the letter n changes the n sound slightly.

kangaroo

Every spring morning the kangaroo and the monkey go to the river bank for a drink.

river bank

Dennis is nervous about going to a new school.

He doesn't know anyone or a single rule.

In the morning Dennis dresses
in a new shirt and jeans.

He brings his notebooks, pencils,
and a snack of long, green beans.

The students listen and learn
about the letter n in English class.

During band, Dennis plays
a French horn made of brass.

In art, Dennis shows off his talent
by drawing a brown kangaroo.

He paints nine bunnies
and everyone sees what he can do.

Moon

Nick and Erin invite Dennis
to join them for lunch at noon.

Then they sit together in science
and learn about the moon.

When Dennis returns home,
his mom wants to know how it went.

Dennis tells her about the friends
he made, and that he is now content!

Which words have
the letter **n**?

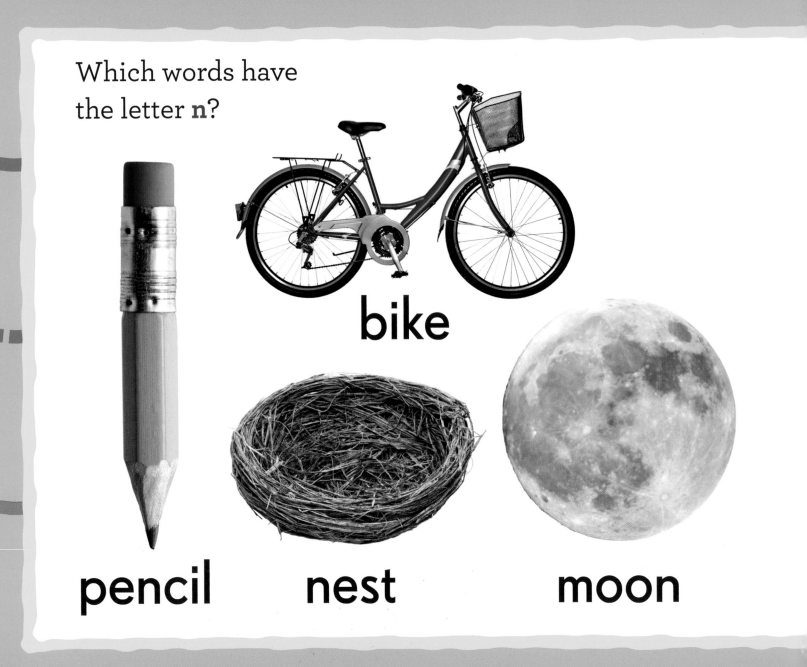

bike

pencil   nest   moon

kangaroo

pajamas

bunny

kite

23

Glossary

bean (p. 16) – a seed or a pod that you can eat.

content (p. 20) – being happy with things the way they are.

French horn (p. 17) – a musical instrument with a coiled tube that you play by blowing into a mouthpiece on one end.

inn (p. 12) – a small hotel.

nibble (p. 7) – to eat using small bites.

noodles (pp. 6, 7) – pasta that is shaped into strips, such as spaghetti.

noon (p. 19) –12 o'clock in the middle of the day.

notebook (p. 16) – a small pad of paper used for writing and drawing.

science (p. 19) – the study and knowledge of the natural world and the events that occur in it.

To promote letter recognition, letters are highlighted instead of glossary words in this series. The page numbers above indicate where the glossary words can be found.

More Words with **N**

Find the **n** in the beginning, middle, or end of each word.

again	end	need	noise	one
barn	hand	never	nose	only
been	money	nice	not	plant
candy	name	night	number	queen
down	nap	no	nurse	van
elephant	near	nobody	nut	woman

HELLO my name is Nancy